To and For All Law Enforcement
This is the 24th Helper!

This has been put together especially for you!

Now can we at least put aside all
biases and prejudices to receive peace?

Cleveland can give the world a positive sight to see!

This booklet is dedicated to the police in conjunction with the book *A Peace Offering for the People and the Police*.

The bottom line is the people are not as reception as the law enforcement agencies about a plan and people generally go with the flow and it is a wish with a large amount of hope that comes along with it, that you, being first, would ignite an urge that the average citizen would want to be a part of this way in making history.

We should take this information on
a common sense basis!

The Lord is still Almighty So let's do This

- First, we want to be on one accord and we have proposed that if you are in Cleveland, we the people would like you to think of our home as the City of motherly and fatherly love.

- Second, we are hoping you become deputized on a spiritual presence of holiness that gives you a supernatural presence of thinking that

1

brings out the power of love so all in your presence will be affected to want to feel the need to do the right thing.

- Third, we wish a different kind of blessing falls upon you and all the protesters as if the bridge that can be crossed is filled with people who have the same kind of nature of love in them as the people who crossed the bridge in Selma, Alabama.

- Fourth, at the time of the protests may the healing balm of Gilead fall down on the city and people of Cleveland as if the presence of the Lord has grown in strength within all people.

This certifies that there is nothing missing in the training for the law enforcement people. This is a spiritual training program.

Bound to Heaven Publishing/Ministries
Copyright 2016
U.S. Library of Congress

Hello and thank you for your interest. My name is Tracy E. Bush. This is being presented to a select group of individuals who may give toward the cause in order to it to create a peaceful environment in our City. We are looking to raise money to create promotion because this message and others need to be known before the end of June.

This is a message from the now generation who do not just see the possible but does the impossible.

What have I done as a developer, creator or deliverer of a message? Could it be a mathematical code that I have come up with to break down the spiritual elements of fear that removes it from the presence of mankind by looking at it as if it is a particle as other things are made of with a DNA status?

The news I have to share is not all good. The trump has a way of feeding off of people's fear and emotions. He likes to taunt people and make them mad like a kid does when they are bullying someone else. Therefore, he can be considered a man-kid and not like someone else called him a man-baby. In other words, he is like a baby goat which is the true meaning of "kid."

Now, to keep things on the up and up, this material that is included in this package is something that is important enough for all to know who are involved in the upcoming process of politics that will be going on in the City of Cleveland. If you are for trump, to protect yourself also, you need to get the number 24 on your checklist. Don't leave home without it because it will help you if you think about creating harm to someone else. If you are opposed to trump, you need it also.

You can find all of this in some of the books that will be mentioned to you later to help stop the real crook from doing harm.

It is true there are some people who have to have some kind of fear factor in their life so I will go one up on you with a better than fair trade to get a new level of fear try to not fail at becoming a disciple. This book will be on the list also. When some people are caught up in this phase of life, they may follow trouble. If you are, or think you are, a Christian here is a way to get your spirit fired up for the Lord.

The worse part for some is like walking around in a shallow grave that allows a straw in to breathe air because everything else is closed or covered up, meaning the way one thinks and is able to see things. This is called a part of the walking dead sin-drome that the lost are faced with. That is why this spiritual analogy is needed to give an anecdote to freedom, thanks to God. Amen and hallelujah

Today's News to Help Stop Future Blues!

Is the media afraid to announce this in order to stop any outrageous trouble at the RNC? Can the City of Cleveland, Ohio have a reprieve or a way to escape having violence at the RNC? To do this people need to pursue what is known as the 24th Helper, along with the other 23 agencies pursuing safety. Now can last come first and first come last? Get complete information at the website, go to page titled "Stop the Fear."

Now listen up, is there a double standard that is something that is perhaps everyone's fault. Do the media think on a level of no one would believe this anyway? That is how some may feel that others are non-believers with ungodliness as they may be that won't give this a chance because of no faith. Now this is an unfortunate part of reality, but it may exist?

Why do we fear change to a degree we are willing to mash it so others can't have a way to start to hate more people from not seeing things being as well as could be? With the process of no hate comes from the people in Cleveland at the time of the RNC is needed now to do to make this happen.

Everyone in the country that may come to Cleveland, Ohio or an area close to the City to protest should know about this information. This can also work for the DNC. Get complete information at website.

This also may be a kind of plea to go against the grain and make this known all over the country before the convention starts to give it a chance!

If this information gets out in the media then the calling goes out for a few people to become members of the Trojan horse team we can take a few good guys that can lead a way to peace it will be like leading a peace movement in a Godly way not a war as was with the men who came out of the horse in the written story process that may seem or sound the same but it is totally different get the details at on the website.

There is no way around the promotion that
has been placed in this book; it's needed!

News to Keep People Updated
(that people need to know)

To anyone who are going down to protest at the RNC to help assure your safety it only takes one and a half hour, at most, to go over and read the book, _A Guide to Stop Fear and Prevent Problems at the RNC_. If you want the best result that can help show you can get a copy and share it with family and friends! The investment is only $5.43 for a paper back, get it at Createspace Store! This is what can help others.

Cleveland is gearing up with addition blessings to have less problems at the convention. Now they are doing one or more things I hope than Philadelphia, PA, I say this without prejudice. It is using the information supplied by Bro. Tracy Bush. Now to even make it more interesting an open bet has been placed to see whose city has less violence behind the convention. Well the idea is to develop more peace to help assure that no kind of foreign or domestic enemy get a chance to also create trouble or worse do harm to a lot of people. Therefore both Cities need to get on the same page about this! The one goal is safety first for all people!!!!

More About the Author

You can say as some others do that Tracy is gifted by way of the work he does in the causes he affects with it on a positive level. He was born in the backwoods and was delivered by a midwife. He is a self-educated man largely without a high school diploma. He has been a soldier on the battlefield for over 30 years in his street ministry. He has been used by the Lord to do the work of a saint. He has taken on the most difficult tasks that helps to lead others in ways out of the darkness they may be trapped in.

The amazing thing is he has put together a library of help-self work anyone can hire themselves out to get out of an ungodly way of thinking or acting that prepares them for the future to not go down a dark pathway where harm can be waiting on them that gives them insight and hindsight to love the life they live and live the life they love and make change a part of their daily tasks.

To take things one step farther, it also incorporated the balance of spiritual skills. The messages are many the books are created to last much longer than a lifetime with the information of the protesting and politics that can teach you a way to make a way out of no way if it is needed.

What is it that also can be said about Tracy? He is a spiritual bad buster that prevents the unseen wars that help to keep life flowing and moving along.

What is and can be one of the biggest things that the books can and will do for someone is knock down and free people who the devil may have a stronghold on to make them capable of causing trouble. There are other books left to complete that will come in the future as part of the new set of formulas for success. They will include *All Peoples Handbook*, that helps people develop spiritual skills. For more information, go to website.

This Can't be Said Enough!
Is the 24th Helper to the RNC the Last Being First?

We have a reason to get excited about the stopping of a kind of madness and the gift of having a way to replace the negative energy with positive ways to go that redevelops human energy is at hand. If we are the hands of the Lord then we should use this. A part of the blind spot can be seen or it is just time to get the gray out of the way. The world doesn't stop people from having the truth that leads to freedom, people stop themselves. Problems of all kinds can be cleaned up.

Fear of what may happen at the upcoming RNC: Fear of terrorists intruding on our city at the same time because of the convention. Fear of what may happen with a problem between the people and the police they may face at the protests during the RNC. These are only problems people can fix them. The answers are in the books. Do we want to try to fix them before they get broken at least or are we afraid of just trying? I don't think so.

Help add more peace to the city. We are officially adopting a new name for Cleveland, Ohio: the city of motherly and fatherly love! The mayor and council have been informed. One of the reasons we have for doing this is to share the development of a plan provided by Bound to Heaven Publishing/Ministries and predicting that Clevelanders will have no more or less protestors displaying violence than the city of brotherly love.

We have even announced an ongoing similar wager between the cities if the two agree to it and they have been informed. The wager is for the city that experiences the least amount of friction during the time of their respective conventions this summer. The winner would receive a sandwich from the losing city; Philadelphia PA, with a Philly steak versus the famous Cleveland corned beef sandwich. It is all left up the people to apply the love to make this plan of peace work and may God bless us all with it.

The time is here to stop the fear! Let's make Cleveland first.

There is a trend in the world that people are now at odds with. The establishment on many levels and if we can conquer and stop some of the ungodliness that comes with it so why not? We should develop a break before we break up a part of our life. There is not any way we can guarantee a full proof way to stop all violence at any protest or rally. But if we can cut it down dramatically, why not put forth the effort.

Here is all that is offered now. Now if you want to be in the know, get a copy of one or more of the following books: _What Is Going On_? (the negative protest stopper), _"The Devil Passed Me By"_ (a living play you can be a part of), _Ending Political Wars in America_, _A Guide to Stop Fear and Prevent Problems at the RNC_. Get the facts and all you need from A to Z in the guide. _A Promise to Help Prevent Violence at Protests and Rallies in America! Fixing What is Broken in America by Stopping Towerism_. The use of this complete wisdom can help stop ungodliness anywhere. To get more details about the books or to receive a copy in paperback please order it from Creatspace.com eStore or for an eBook go to Amazon.com, search Bro. Tracy Bush. Please help with the promotion we need you. Thank you from Bro. Tracy E. Bush, local author and Cleveland resident. Please visit boundtoheaven.org. We can learn to use an ounce of prevention to detoxify elements that leaves us with a pound of cure!

Do you have the Capacity to Take This in?

Can we preserve some things every once in a while as if it is back in the day when it was so dry they believed in a rain-man who came through for them and it rained to save the day?

I have no one to blame for the one fact that give people peace and that is a fight, because people fight out of most of all fear, that right fear, especially of the unknown foremost. That is why people protest to get change or stop it.

The fear of the RNC has more than one fear and the biggest is not the one that people are not paying the most attention to because the people don't know and it brings out the fight in them because they don't know exactly what they are so frightened of or about.

Now I will or I have listed some things that are mostly unknown that people fill lost to an understanding of what is really going on! I will try to put it in a nutshell that I will also crack for you and read the people their good fortune. It is freedom at the same time from the unseen trap of a spiritual war that fell down to earth after lingering around in a dark space as it is doing while people are waiting for the event to take place that add to them acting up and foolish.

What is my problem now if I know what the people needed, but don't know what it exactly takes to get them to get it, what can I do other than tell them! I don't know what it takes to get you to take the medicine to fix the fear inside of one self with in the soul of mankind that maybe in a kind of anguish from not knowing what is totally wrong with them and some will get pulled in from all over the country to air out their confessions.

That is why they need to get a complete meal of this kind of soul food to give them balance to fill them with wisdom. Then, there will not be anything missing or broken that could be someone's self-worth and something in a person soul that effects their spirit, because it knows things are not right from the way the soul is feeling and wanting to act.

That is also when Satan jumps in to do what he does to cause hell to rise up to draw people into a fight to let off frustration. This is one of the things that pits people against one another. and to know this and the facts behind it can help stop the madness also sadness that unblinds people so they see no reason to fight unless it i fair by showing people how to have the strength to do the right things also in a civilized way.

Thanks to God!

If we turn our backs on this that could be a warning some of us may not live to regret.

What is my biggest concern? It is that so many people with towerism or are affected by it, are going to be gathered in one place, in the City of Cleveland, Ohio. The politicians are one of the larger groups of people in the world who have this and they don't identify with it.

You may say what does this have to do with anything? Foremost, who hates Americans? Most terrorists and they hate politicians who are towerists. To give you a vision of a single thought, they took down the twin towers to stop the process of the economy, they thought, as well as trying to hit the

Pentagon and another place in order to cripple the USA.

Now do they have the biggest rattling noise ever that is one of the people now as a towerist that is attracting terrorists to the country, namely Trump? We do and we can do something about it. We can do this by exposing the truth that causes the unknown fear to help free people from this unknown power that does exist, even though we can't see or smell it but it offends the Lord's nostrils. He has shared that with me and that is upsetting the people. We can put a stop to it by showing up with love and letting people know we understand now the important thing. That is to let them know you understand what they need to know and then share it with them to bring about peace.

To make it clearer look at the way a person is thinking without any bias take Trump and if he stops acting like a wanna-be man-baby and get his problem of being a towerist fixed, the people who are following him that are trumpees need a trumpectomy to free them from a kind of spell they are under with a way of understanding that gives light because they may feel like they are lost in a cave. I have explained this in the books I write.

There is such thing as a man-child. They have a different way about their life and thinking than a man-baby. That has nothing to do with a Godly child as is the opposite in both cases. To clear things up even more, a man-baby doesn't cut it as a mature person in the real world when it comes down to worldly affairs and politics.

To reveal something about myself: I am and was a man-child all of my life and I have met some man-babies and in one way they were foolish in one way or another. One of the reasons is because of selfishness and the refusal to accept becoming a real child of the Lord.

It seems as if the perfect storm is brewing and the City has everything it wants because it has everything going for itself even the sports teams. The City is on a winning streak so why not add the one other message of protection that adds up to more love to be shown. With the helper no. 24 it can't hurt if the people want and need the wisdom in their time of distress to clear a pathway for peace!

This Creates Therapy for All People

To the police: find a song then sing it at a right time to show love on the human side of who you are. This may help create peace to make people think and stop them from building up frustration gets help. Have churches around the bridge and downtown to ring their bells. That's right, do something different that takes people's minds off of them wanting to cause trouble they want freedom from, that is troubling them and they may be not be completely aware of it.

The thinking behind this is if we the people behind the god created concept of peace in a new way since the same old ways don't work that well. Therefore, if we at Bound to Heaven Publishing/Ministries cannot get the people that are going to be out in the crowds that are protesting, we can at least put the law enforcement agencies on the same page to help stop the earthly presence of a demonic spirit that falls onto people from the unseen spiritual war that is taking place when a great discrepancy is taking place between two set of people that happens in darkness but is now brought to light. It will in return stop lots of trouble from happening.

1. Matthew 5:9 Blessed are the peacemakers, for they shall be called sons of God!

2. Share this with your spouse;

3. Pray for this ideology to come to pass with the Lord's favor.

To learn more about what I am talking about with spirituality, you will have to get more information from other books that I have authored.

The other cities that are not going to be helping to head off any trouble at the RNC may be the ones that are the real losers if it turns out to be not as bad as some may think it is going to be, thanks to a new level of help that the Lord can supply.

Now if everything works out the protesters that don't want trouble will stay on the side of the law. Time will tell how sweet it is to be loved by the Lord.

At BTHPM, we will find a way to have a number of churches open for baptism people 24/7 if needed or if needed we can set something at the Lake at Edgewater. We will have kite flying groups signs of good news all over.

I have a GoFundMe account to help me keep working on making America great. Please make donations at www.gofundme.com/nzp42cys. Foremost, to put my new spiritual skills learning center open once again. I have written many over 30 books that will be made free to readers who can't buy them, but do not have the money to promote them to make a living off of. Please help. You may visit my website www.boundtoheaven.org, for further information.

If there are any questions, or if you would like to know more about Bro. Bush and any of the projects of the ministry, please send email to tb.bthpm@gmail.com.

Bro. Bush has received many endorsements from local clergy as well as public service individuals.

No one needs to walk into a perfect storm without a Godly plan or solution if there is one available.

The placement of the information may seem all over the place but once you let it all set in you will see the whole growth process.

This book is priceless and no dollar quote can compare to its real worth. Therefore, give as much as you would give to an offering at a house that is made of love because it was made and came from love.

The first people we want to give a break to have little or nothing to do with the RNC. It is all people in the medical field and community at hospitals. Let's give them a break everyone; they work hard enough.

The books help stop the crook, Satan from trying to steal some of the people's joy. Now, if I said a miracle can come in a book if you took time to learn of it, would you? That may be the next most important thing as the Christmas story of Cleveland. But, this is a blessing that may have been chosen to become a part of making history from the state of peace we can display.

If you know that outside police officers and others show them some love, send them a copy of this and the other books that can help the team. We all have time enough to pat ourselves on the back, but that too has a time and place that can come in the month of August.

We can all help to keep the people and city safe and stop the setbacks of madness and sadness with our love coming together as one. Can this be a kind of life jacket for the city? I think so, how about you?

We at BTHPM are giving honor to the people in a new book that will be coming out in the fall of 2016 titled, *The Wisdom to Keep the Blood Blue*.

Now to add the additional insurance the lord provides.

Once the seeds of this wisdom is planted and it start to sprout the growth is immediate with the mind and heart that will be filled with a heavenly presence that can stop the emotions that are attached to an ungodly state of being. That state of being prefers war and harm over peace. Therefore, don't fear the new you with the armor that is the kind that a real servant of mankind needed to wear! It will be placed upon you for you to have on daily. It can keep things safe and most of all the spirit within will become a blessing to them and others. Growth time of exhibiting the process of change 24 to 72 hours may be the norm, but if the heart is already there it can occur in a twinkling of an eye.

Got Skills? If Not, Get Skills

Stopping one of the worse things in the world that people are affected with, that is being dim-witted. Do not get with it; escape from it. How can this be done? It is with father wit and mother wit. It comes with the development of spiritual skills. Get skills, get witted up. It is like a new and fresh way of thinking that adds to life.

If we get a city full of people on that level, there is going to be less crime, less sin, with a better chance to make it in life. Now, let's create blessings and pass on luck. It does not have anything to do with much but the buck. The blessings we create can fulfill a lifetime of dreams and a person only needs one good dream and as a song I wrote goes, one dream, one dream, we are blessed just to have one dream.

Your Time is Important:

This Brief Information Hopes to Give You What You Need to Help You Make up Your Mind to Help

This is a part of the plan the Lord has put together for law enforcement. Your positive energy and your family prayers will be working together as a wall around the protesters who are lost out of reality, who are in the center. Now as the police officers stand guard to protect the innocent civilians and the City from any harm of people or property.

The negativity will get snuffed out peacefully or smoothed out by positive energy and if some of the people in the middle are on the right spiritual level by being enlightened. This can be done with one or more of the books I have to help quench the fire Satan wants to serve up.

The test run for all of this was done last year at what could have been a messy protest. I attended this protest to test the waters with A Peace Offering and it helped cool things off. Why not expect the same results or better because there was not an explosion of violence and chaos and that is what we are stopping through the methodology we are using. Let's do this. God has given us a plan so let's make it work. He does not want to do everything for us. He wants us to learn to make a miracle appear in our lifetime. If you say, "what does God have to do with this?" When we make him happy we make ourselves happy!

Get Yourself in the Right Position

The books for the police are: 1. *To and For All Law Enforcement: this is the 24th Helper*; 2. *A Peace Offering for the People and the Police*; and 3. *The Devil Passed Me By*.

The books for the people are: 1. *A Guide to Stop Fear and Prevent Problems at the RNC*; 2. *A Promise to Help Prevent Violence at Protests and Rallies in America!*; 2. *What's Going On?*; and 3. *The Devil Passed Me By*.

The books for the politicians are: 1. *Ending Political Wars in America*; 2. *Fixing What is Broken in America* by *Stopping Towerism*; and 3. *The Recovery of the U.S. Government (The Beginning)*.

Finally, the book for all three groups of people is titled, *Ending Spiritual Warfare in America!*

All of the newer books that are talked about are only available at Amazon.com, search Bro. Tracy Bush. To help the cause more please purchase them from Createspace.com estore. One of the books at this time, the 24th Helper can only be purchased off of the information on the website until further notice – the time when it can be ordered online will be announced soon.

This is truly a peace dance that we can do to stop the nonsense that can take place.

What is the real inside scoop? If we stop the spiritual warfare that is taking place now that creates fear, we win one of the battles. Therefore, when we are confronted with the second earthly one, we are in a better place to have peace and both sides will have the right self-confidence that won't get out of hand. That way there won't be a fight, maybe there won't even be a scrimmage. This will create the scenario and effect of the devil passing the people by. It won't hurt to read all the books to give your spirit a better way to connect with other people spiritually. This is a part of what love can do for me and you.

Do not be too cheap to change. Pay the cost to be the boss of your spiritual life, with getting the wisdom you need to carry the cross you have to shoulder on your own.

As a nation of people we have to come together more. If we stand together and not divided the real enemy cannot attack us at one of our weakest points. Now is the time to use the pen of wisdom as a sword with two edges; one for Satan and one to keep away the individuals he may send to commit a sin upon the people and land. Together we stand, divided we fall. Try something new, it cannot hurt and look what may be saved, a great American way that we can fix.

This concludes a brief presentation if you have any more time to keep reading it is hoped your time was and will be well spent!

Big Jump Up In Life For All In Cleveland, OH
We Can Help Philadelphia, Pa Too!!

I am confident that there will be anywhere from a 50%- 70% decrease in potential violence, harm or danger. The more people who join in the more successful things will be.

Always and Forever

The visions for all people to have in their heart: can there only be one saved at any kind of gathering or will Satan take all?

You can suggest or speculate whether this maybe right or wrong but you will have to help by reading into a kind of living goal mind of love. Then act with faith people to get your way out of a kind of hell hole that has been dug for people because of the lack of spiritual wisdom in a process of growth.

Stopping a child-like towerist is or may be somewhat devilish in a presence that wants to be a greater than life person who is a foolish spirit that has gotten a sickness in them that only the Lord can fix if they let him and no one should ignore them!

The people with towerism are coming to Cleveland and this is a real problem. Are we ready? No, if we do not know how to help them resign themselves to end their problems. This is really what is going on. Fighting with the power of police and jail cells is not the real answer. It is a spiritual fight to be won first and everything else will fix itself. We do this by helping people with towerism take a look at themselves and the baggage they are carrying around and what they have to do to fix it because they are locked into something they do not know about. If we miss this point on unveiling a part of history, it can be left undone forever. The problem that people have is that Satan developed a distraction to take over one's mind and soul away from the truth to be known and told about people who have harmed others and the world.

The sickness of towerism must be exposed to get it fixed. The smoke screen is madness and sadness Satan keeps using to blind people to the truth. Get the truth, get Satan smoked out of people's way and stop the conflict and fighting at the same time. Then show prayers work by people exposing the miracles of it all that comes to light.

One of the worse things that can happen is not showing people with towerism how to plant the right seeds in their garden of self to stop the problem they have. Along with this people are to help by first knowing what is going on with this inside scoop of news that says the problem of the people fighting takes away from the process of growth that people have been locked into who are in chains of the government.

We as the people have to do our part and fix some things ourselves to give them a chance to fix themselves. We can learn to stop fighting among one another at this kind of gathering at the RNC or DNC and if they see that it gives them a chance to stop fighting with each other also.

It is like a trickle up affect but we the people must become the leaders and they will follow. The process of a new way of growth is not new but the people forgot to use it. Let the people set a good example at any upcoming protests in Cleveland. The country will stop and see a new pathway out of a kind of hell hole that Satan is trying to continually put us in so we have an outlook as if we are as bad as a part of the rest of the world would like to think we are. Some may have good reason and they see us as terrorists to them. It is only because we have a problem with the people who have towerism.

It is time to mend the brokenness that we have as a people. It is the land of the free and home of the brave that is on the march to do that but we must face up to our own idiosyncrasies or foolish ways first.

Therefore, learn what is needed to stop the bloodshed at home with the heartfelt messages that are here for you. For this event, everyone gets to have a little Mohammed Ali in them being a humanitarian and not a fighter. Are you a part of this new peaceful rising up against Satan that breaks the chain that he puts on people's soul no matter what color they are? The time has come for a new level of freedom for the American people. I personally give thanks, saying hallelujah and praise the Lord.

As author and messenger, I am not able to do any more than what I have already done without a financial gift to help pay for the things that is needed. Your help is needed. Please be a God send to me, I am trying to be one to you.

I need the money to keep getting the message out. If you don't feel this is worth the donation I will give your money back because this is worth more than anyone could pay for actually.

The one thing I need to do I don't like but I have no way around it. It may seem I am speaking in the third person.

People need to stop reinventing ways to impose their pain on to someone else to take a bite out of crime that also stops sin in its tracks. This is the next to the best tools the police can have to fight crime and that is love.

What the Lord has given us can't
be taken away but we must use it or lose it.

Don't forget the best way to prepare for war is to be
prepared for peace.

Turning a time of a kind of Pentecost cost into
pennies of cost compared to a real cost.

This may be one of the most important documents that is related to the RNC that can help make a way to increase the peace. The police need a peace offering made to and for them before they go into this kind of battle that will stop the spiritual war that Satan wants to trap them in.

A Thought

If the people in the crowd that police were controlling knew what you have learned from this book, how would both of you act? It is with respect and love I would think.

I am confident that there will be anywhere from a 50%- 70% decrease in potential violence, harm or danger. The more people who join in the more successful things will be.

You can suggest or speculate whether this maybe right or wrong but you will have to help by reading into a kind of living goal mind of love. Then act with faith people to get your way out of a kind of hell hole that has been dug for people because of the lack of spiritual wisdom in a process of growth.

If anyone wants to receive more copies, please send a donation of at least $6.50, per copy, payable to Tracy E. Bush, to Post Office Box 605301, Cleveland, Ohio 44105.

When you read the little book with a big bite, think of yourself on the same level as a reader with a guardian angel to let you know what is right, if you don't think you know.

One of the goals is to win one-half of the potential upcoming battle and stop another kind of war that can and may have even worse results.

The producer of this and all of the other information is not a business that is in any shape to be able to afford to give this good news away for free, we need your help. If we can come up with a way to help curve violence in any way, shape or form it is a priceless thing to be used and thankful for because it is a gift from the Lord.

In saying all of this, it is worth the cost of labor put into it to produce it and the supply of paper and ink it takes also. What could this be called? A labor of love that is calling out to be known by as many people as it can. The love is free. The way the love needs to be spread around costs.

After reading this, if there is anyone who feels like I do at times when you are in need of knowing that there is someone else who needs to know what you are thinking because they may be thinking the same thing, share it so no one feels alone.

Philippians 4:17
17. Not that I seek the gift, but I seek the fruit that abounds to your account.

Acts 20:24
24. But none of these things move me; nor do I count my life dear to myself, so that I may finish my race with joy, and the ministry which I received from the Lord Jesus, to testify to the gospel of the grace of God.